Stray Kids

HERE TO STAY

KATY SPRINKEL

TRIUMPH
BOOKS

CONTENTS

CHAPTER 1

New Kids on the Block

Are Stray Kids the next big thing in pop music?

Maybe so; the numbers don't lie. The explosive octet from South Korea—featuring members Bang Chan, Lee Know, Changbin, Hyunjin, Han, Felix, Seungmin, and I.N—has already found considerable crossover success in the U.S., where the group's last four album releases landed them atop Billboard's Artist 100 chart. That achievement was fueled by their ardent and ever-expanding group of fans, known collectively as STAY, which has cemented Stray Kids as a formidable power player in the global music landscape.

Founded in 2017, Stray Kids (abbreviated SKZ) have steadily been building an international fan base through direct fan engagement, strategic positioning, and continuous music production. It's a success story that has earned them comparisons to another K-pop group: global juggernaut BTS. While enthusiasm for K-pop has been building over the last decades, it was BTS that put it on the map in the United States. And with BTS on hiatus as of the summer of 2023, many believe Stray Kids are poised to step into that spotlight.

Comparisons of the two groups were inevitable, but Stray Kids is nothing like BTS—or any K-pop artist, for that matter. Though they are on the roster of JYPE, one of the longtime Big Three major labels in Korea, Stray Kids have managed to carve out a particular niche for themselves by bucking the standard conventions so typical in the K-pop musical apparatus. For one, leader Bang Chan was allowed to choose the members who make up the group. And from the very beginning, this group has written, arranged, and produced their own musical output. If that doesn't sound particularly impressive, consider

this: they're the first ones ever to do it in JYPE's history.

Stray Kids' unique composition translates to their music, which touches on a wide variety of genres including EDM, trance, R&B, pop, hip-hop, and industrial. It's a mash-up all their own, sometimes described as "noisy" K-pop. They occupy a space in music that is free from inhibition and at essence a reflection of their own distinct and disparate personalities. And their high-energy, highly technical performances have thrilled audiences from the first.

By any measure, 2023 was a banner year for the group, which saw them achieve a number of superlatives. They eclipsed 5 billion streams on Spotify that

STRAY KiDS 101

- The band debuted in 2017 after appearing on JYP Entertainment's reality survival show *Stray Kids*.

- Originally a nine-man outfit, member Woojin left the group in 2019.

- The group is led by Bang Chan, who collaborated with bandmates Changbin and Han under the name 3RACHA before choosing the members who would form the larger group.

- Stray Kids consists of three subgroups—3RACHA: Bang Chan, Changbin, and Han, who produce and compose most of the group's songs; DanceRacha: the group's main dancers, Lee Know, Hyunjin, and Felix; and VocalRacha: the group's main singers, Seungmin and I.N.

- Their last four albums have hit No. 1 on the Billboard Top Album Sales charts, cementing them as one of the all-time most successful K-pop acts in the U.S.

- The group's nickname is the abbreviated SKZ.

- The group's fan base is known as STAY (dropping the R from *Stray*), and their motto is, "You make Stray Kids Stay."

year, and their full-length album, *5-Star*, became the most preordered album in K-pop history. In fact, they are the second-most-streamed K-pop group of all time (after, you guessed it, BTS). Back at home, leader Bang Chan became the third-most-copyrighted songwriter in K-pop history for his prodigious output. Stray Kids achieved Penta-Million Seller status, and tickets for a fan meeting at the huge KSPO Dome in Seoul sold out in *minutes*. They sold out venue after venue on their 2023 world tour, played Lollapalooza Paris and the Global Citizen Festival, and performed at the MTV VMAs and Billboard Music Awards, further strengthening their international credentials.

Set to embark on another world tour in 2024 and with multiple musical projects in progress, Stray Kids are poised to have their biggest year yet. With their sights trained on even greater heights, they're ready to heed STAY's call for "total world domination."

Not yet a member of STAY? Read on for everything you need to know about Stray Kids before the group lands at an arena near you. You'll learn about the band's formation; their music, choreography, and visuals; their relationship with their fan base; and lots of details about each of SKZ's eight members. But first, a brief history lesson about the dazzling, wonderful world of K-pop. ⬤

CHAPTER 2

The Korean Wave

To the outside observer,

K-pop looks like a sugarcoated confection, a frenetic collection of beats, catchy hooks, super-sharp dancing, and kaleidoscopic visuals performed by impossibly attractive singers and entertainers. But to dismiss it as a cotton-candy version of pop music would be way off the mark. Not only is K-pop wide-ranging in its musical styles and onstage product, it's serious business. Big business.

In fact, it is nearly impossible to overestimate the power of K-pop. The multibillion-dollar industry (that's right, *billion* with a *B*) is one of South Korea's biggest exports, and a huge contributor to the country's bottom line. Those eye-popping numbers are pretty impressive considering South Korea is only the 29th-largest country in the world but the world's 6th-largest market for recorded music by revenue, according to the International Federation of the Phonographic Industry.

What's surprising is that K-pop itself is a fairly new phenomenon. Well into the 1980s, cultural conservatism in South Korea was considerably strict. "Standards" such as short haircuts on

Cross Gene performs on *Show Champion*.

men and modest hemlines on women's clothing were the norm. Additionally, the government controlled the media, so all radio and television programming was under its thumb. The end result in music was an especially bland mixture of inoffensive, by-the-numbers pop music alongside traditional Korean music, known as *trot* (short for *foxtrot*).

When South Korea became a democracy in 1987, the rules started to relax a little bit. One of the most popular television formats in South Korea at that time was the musical competition show, and remains so today. Forebears to Western programs such as *American Idol* and *The Voice*, Korea's weekly music shows—such as *Inkigayo*, *Show Champion*, and *Music Bank*— were nothing less than appointment

Seo Taiji and Boys in the early 1990s.

DID YOU KNOW?

Korean is one of the fastest-growing languages in the world. According to the language training site Duolingo, Korean is its seventh-most-studied language program and the second-most-popular Asian language (trailing Japanese by a razor-thin margin). And the Modern Language Association reported that enrollments in college-level Korean courses in the U.S. have more than doubled in the past two decades.

television. (And in a country where 99 percent of homes had a TV, that was major.) Audiences were (and remain) hugely invested in the outcomes.

Enter Seo Taiji and Boys. On April 11, 1992, the trio performed on the MBC network's live weekly talent show. Influenced by the new jack swing style popularized by American artists Bell Biv DeVoe and Bobby Brown, among others, their song "Nan Arayo" was completely

> **"There may be no more unlikely pop-culture success in the world right now than South Korean *hallyu*."**
> —*Wall Street Journal*

Seoul's K-Star Road, a popular tourist attraction for K-pop fans.

out of left field. The band didn't win the competition—in fact, they came in dead last—but they did something far more lasting: they lit the spark that ignited the K-pop explosion. Their performance had a profound effect on musicians who began to expand their sound beyond the predictable, staid formula popular in South Korea at the time. And by all counts, that 1992 performance is considered to be the official beginning of K-pop as we know it today.

When the Asian financial crisis swept across the continent in 1997, South Korea appeared to be on the brink of bankruptcy. Then-president Kim Dae-jung made a bold move, investing heavily in South Korea's entertainment industry and exporting its creative work to save the country from collapse. The gambit worked. Korean music became popular in China as soon as it hit the airwaves there. And when Korean shows landed on Japanese television screens, viewers couldn't get enough. International audiences' obsession with Korean entertainers had an enormous ripple effect, and the craze for all things Korean became all-encompassing.

They call it *hallyu*—the Korean wave— and it describes the influence of Korean culture on consumers. It encompasses not just music but television and movies, business, fashion, beauty, and even cuisine. (It sounds outlandish, but it's not inaccurate to say that the international rise in popularity of K-pop and Korean television (K-drama) has created opportunities for people around the world to buy Samsung phones and get kimchi at their local grocery stores.) The term *hallyu* was initially coined by Chinese journalists looking to describe the immense effect Korean culture was having on Chinese pop culture. The word was subsequently adopted by the South Korean government as a badge of honor and a tool for promoting both industry and tourism.

Today, the wave of *hallyu* is stronger than ever, as Korean imports have gained a foothold around the globe. ⬤

A Seoul vendor selling K-pop and K-drama merchandise.

"No one can stop Stray Kids. They are on an upward trajectory and show no signs of slowing down."

—Teen Vogue

GREAT MoMENTS iN HALLYU
American Edition

1994: *All-American Girl*, created by and starring comedienne Margaret Cho, premieres on ABC. It was the first major network show to feature an East Asian family at its center.

2003: *A Tale of Two Sisters* is the first Korean-language horror film to be released in U.S. theaters, kicking off a K-horror craze. (An English-language remake, *The Uninvited*, would be released in 2009.)

2007: The son of Korean immigrants, chef David Chang wins his first James Beard Award en route to becoming one of the most influential chefs in the nation.

2009: Seoul-based Samsung releases its first Galaxy smartphone to U.S. retailers.

2012: The first KCON is held in the U.S., allowing fans to get up close and personal with their favorite K-pop artists.

2012: Psy's "Gangnam Style" sweeps the nation, becoming the most watched video in YouTube history, a title it holds for five years.

2019: Bong Joon-Ho's *Parasite* wins the Academy Award for Best Picture, just the second foreign language film (after France's silent film *The Artist*, in 2012) to win the prize in the awards' nearly century-long history.

2020: BTS blows up the Billboard Hot 100 with "Dynamite," the first-ever K-pop song to debut at the chart's top spot.

2021: Korean import *Squid Game* becomes a runaway success on Netflix.

2021: Youn Yuh-jung wins Best Supporting Actress for her role in *Minari*, making her the first Korean actor to take home the prestigious movie award.

2023: Stray Kids' *Rock-Star* storms the Billboard charts, handing the Stray Kids their fourth No. 1 album in the span of a year and a half.

CHAPTER 3

The K-Pop Machine

Seo Taiji and Boys might not have received immediate acclaim for their innovation, but no one could say they didn't get attention. Their 1992 performance of "Nan Arayo" polarized audiences, who had never before seen a mash-up of Korean and American music. They were sharply criticized by some, who objected to their use of hip-hop beats and rhythms (now the stock in trade of K-pop). They also committed such unforgivable sins as sporting dreadlocked hair and wearing bleached and ripped jeans.

Still, despite such offenses, "Nan Arayo" ultimately became a huge hit at home—it reigned for 17 weeks as the No. 1 song in the country—establishing them as a massive idol group in the process. They rode a tidal wave of success in the following four years, all the while experimenting with a wide range of musical styles, from hip-hop and rap styles popular over the American airwaves at that time to the softer, sweeter R&B balladeering of U.S. artists such as K-Ci & JoJo and Babyface.

The reason why Seo Taiji and Boys are considered the first K-pop band is that they literally blew up the system. Generally speaking, fans

Red Velvet appears at the Gaon Chart Music Awards in 2022.

don't really consider K-pop to be a genre of music, because there's no one identifiable sound. Korean groups are characteristically open to experimentation and changing their style, mashing up different influences. It's all about the full experience: the music, the live performances, the videos, the variety/competition shows, and the physical packaging of the musical product. Before K-pop, music was ostensibly minted by the broadcasting companies, which promoted their own on-air products. But this group wrote, produced, and choreographed everything on their own. And because of their success, they upended the status quo. A new studio production company system was born.

When the band broke up in 1996, one of the "Boys"—Yang Hyun-suk—joined the fray, founding YG Entertainment (YG comes from his nickname, Yang-gun).

The YG label is one of the so-called Big Three entertainment companies in Korea. Along with SM Entertainment and JYP Entertainment (founded by former idol Jin-young Park), they dominate the musical landscape in Korea. Together, they produce the lion's share of K-pop music, and their reach is enormous. (And in recent years, Big Hit has ascended as well—turning the Big Three into the Big Four—thanks in large part to their biggest artist, BTS.)

Ask any K-pop fan, and they could tell you about each label's hallmarks. Listeners are loyal to their chosen label, much as sports fans stay true to their team's colors. JYPE, the label that is home to Stray Kids, is known for its polished trainee program and diverse class of recruits, turning out some of the most well-rounded musicians of the bunch. SM is known for its performance-oriented focus (big visuals, sharp choreography, and catchy, danceable tunes are its focus). And YG, like its founder, produces artists who tend to push musical barriers and who possess an edgier look than their competitors. Big Hit is known for its highly produced

and polished product, from songwriting to visuals.

Rather than focusing on grooming a select number of artists for long-term success, these companies churn out a multitude of acts, a seemingly revolving door for bands. The metrics for success are simply different in the K-pop system, where a band's shelf life may only be two years. This span is dictated by a couple things: First, the emphasis on youth. Since image is an essential component of the K-pop look, many artists age out of the system quickly. And for boy groups, things are also complicated by a national obligation for all male citizens in South Korea to serve two years in the military, entering a draft at age 18.

Performers start early, auditioning as young as 9 or 10 years old. Foreign language fluency is prized among trainees, and native English speakers are a sought-after commodity. Once individuals are recruited by an agency and signed to long-term contracts, their formal training begins. Children are schooled during the day—a curriculum

> **"K-pop has the power to unite people around the world."**
>
> —Jungkook of BTS

29

that includes a heavy dose of foreign language training, particularly Chinese, Japanese, and English. Then, once the school day is over, students start their music training—singing, dancing, and even media training. This lifestyle is not for the faint of heart; a typical day begins early in the morning and stretches until 8:00 or 9:00 p.m., before students return to their dormitories to complete their day's homework.

Performers spend years as trainees before they are finally brought to market, only coming out once they have mastered their performances down to every hand gesture and eye wink. No detail is overlooked. But the breakneck pace doesn't let up any after their debut. Groups tour extensively, promote exhaustively, and are often tabbed for endorsement deals that require appearances and other promotional efforts. As Tiffany Chan writes on Medium.com, "These South Korean stars represent much more than their latest album...they uphold the image of an ideal in South Korean society, perfectly in-sync choreography, strong vocal talent, and exceptionally attractive visuals."

The music companies also take charge of creating and distributing fan chants, which are another essential part of the live shows. Fans will have what amounts to a script. Instead of vocal backing tracks, live performances are enhanced by precisely crafted audience chants. Most songs have such accompaniments, and they make regular callbacks look like child's play. These fan chants are discussed and dissected obsessively by online fan communities.

Then there's the music. Groups are expected to release songs early and often. In contrast to the American record industry, groups announce their releases a few weeks in advance, drop an EP or album, then start the process all over again. Typically, a K-pop group will release music throughout the calendar year.

90%

Calling it a global phenomenon is no exaggeration. According to industry expert and website K-Pop Radar, almost 90 percent of K-pop listeners live outside South Korea.

Girl group NewJeans performs onstage at Chicago's Lollapalooza Festival in 2023.

And that music is almost always accompanied by a music video, an integral part of the K-pop formula. These videos are invariably lavishly produced affairs that feature the requisite come-hither stares (known in Korean as *aegyo*) from idol group members but also showcase the groups' onstage prowess. The past two decades gave rise to countless idol groups, to whom Stray Kids owes tribute.

The global shift in the music industry in the Information age has been a huge part of K-pop's modern-day success story, which is fueled in large part by the internet. No artist saw greater proof of that than Psy, whose humorous video

SHINee in a 2013 *Show Champion* appearance.

for "Gangnam Style" set seemingly unsurpassable records on YouTube, reaching 1 billion views in record time to become the most watched video by a huge margin. Six years later, with the streaming site *the* undisputed platform for accessing music videos, it's still the fourth-most-watched video of all time.

Since K-pop's introduction in the 1990s, there have been four distinct generations that are widely recognized among the K-pop masses.

The first generation of K-pop was a drastic departure from anything listeners had heard before. Highly political in nature, it addressed the pressures and societal expectations young people felt in South Korea at that time. Though there was no one musical style, the music veered away from the super-sweet Korean pop music that preceded it.

The second generation is considered the golden age of K-pop, and kicked off the Korean Wave across the globe. These second-gen artists brought the rise of the K-pop idol and an organized trainee system to develop talent. Its earmarks are glossy visuals and an emphasis on catchy hooks.

K-pop's third generation took the genre to global heights. Spurred by artists who had been seasoned in the trainee system, its music spanned a number of styles but took a turn away from frivolity and back to more serious themes, including mental health and self-love. Social media played a central role in this period, connecting fans to their idols like never before.

COVID-19 loomed large over those in the fourth generation, who found new ways to connect with their fans through social media efforts, produced content, and virtual concerts. In addition to the traditional boys' and girls' groups, this period also saw the rise of many artists pursuing solo careers after group success. Among the artists to emerge from this period, Stray Kids have found success in large part due to their departure from the traditional conventions of their predecessors. From their unique origins to their musical output, Stray Kids stands out from the crowd. ●

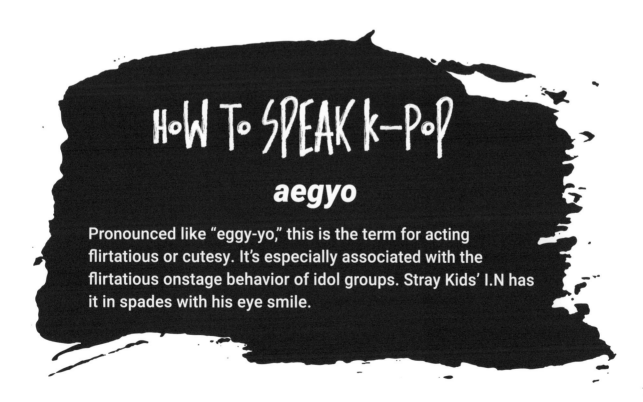

HoW To SPEAK k-PoP

aegyo

Pronounced like "eggy-yo," this is the term for acting flirtatious or cutesy. It's especially associated with the flirtatious onstage behavior of idol groups. Stray Kids' I.N has it in spades with his eye smile.

K-POP FAMILY ALBUM

First Generation (1992–2004)

SEO TAIJI AND BOYS
These guys were true revolutionaries. Not only are they recognized as the originators of K-pop, but their influence helped relax strict censorship laws in Korea, paving the way for the artists to follow.

H.O.T.
K-pop's first idol group, H.O.T. (short for High-Five of Teenagers) consisted of five members and served as the template for the successful boy groups that would follow.

S.E.S.
Taking their name from their members' respective initials (Shoo, Eugene, and Sea), they were considered to be the female counterpart to H.O.T. and the first successful girl group in the genre.

RAIN
After his group Fanclub disbanded, Rain struck out as a solo artist. He went on to become a major celebrity as a singer/songwriter/producer/actor in his home country, where he's known as the Justin Timberlake of Asia.

Second Generation (2005–11)

SHINEE
Nicknamed the Princes of K-Pop, the trendsetting group was known for its high-energy performances and extremely technical and complex choreography.

GIRLS' GENERATION
This nine-member girl group (which became an eight-member group when Jessica left in 2014) made history when they appeared on *The Late Show with David Letterman* in 2012, making them the first K-pop group ever to appear on a U.S. late-night talk show.

SUPER JUNIOR
This massive group—at one point, 13 members!—helped establish the K-pop norm of subunits (divisions within the band that specialize in different aspects of the creative and performance process). They were also the first to break into the Mandarin language market, with a Chinese member among their ranks.

BIGBANG
They called themselves the Kings of K-Pop, and they had the receipts. One of the highest-grossing acts of their generation, the four-man roster—comprised of G-Dragon, T.O.P, Taeyang, and Daesung—were best known for their writing and rap skills.

PSY
Psy's "Gangnam Style" put K-pop on the map in America. The music video literally broke the internet, exceeding the view limit put in place by YouTube programmers and halting the view count at more than 2 billion. (Estimates put that number at roughly 5 billion today.)

Third Generation (2012–19)

BTS
No group can lay more claim to furthering K-pop's global ascendance than the Bangtan Boys and their multitude of record-breaking achievements. The septet of RM, Jin, Suga, J-Hope, Jimin, V, and Jungkook are household names around the world.

BLACKPINK
Featuring members Jennie, Rosé, Lisa, and Jisoo, BLACKPINK is the gold standard of girl groups. American fans are familiar with their music, including bangers such as "Boombayah" and "Ddu-du Ddu-du," the latter of which smashed YouTube records to become the second-most-viewed K-pop video of all time, after Psy's "Gangnam Style."

TWICE
This nine-member girl group debuted after appearing on the Korean competition show *Sixteen*. They won Billboard's Women in Music Breakthrough Artist award in 2023 and are poised to grow their fandom (known collectively as ONCE) exponentially.

RED VELVET
This girl group's music explores a fascinating dual concept. Their "red" music celebrate the bright, fun side, with bouncy, pop-inflected songs, while the "velvet" side tackles more serious subject matter, often in the form of ballads. To date, they've been one of the most successful girl groups stateside.

Fourth Generation (2020–present)

ITZY
Known for their catchy lyrics and incredible dancing talent, this quintet is one of the leading groups on today's K-pop scene.

TXT
Short for Tomorrow and Together, this five-member group is following in the footsteps of labelmates BTS. They appeared at Lollapalooza in 2022 and 2023.

NEWJEANS
They became the first K-pop girl group to hit the Billboard Hot 100 when their "Super Shy" cracked the chart in August 2023.

STRAY KIDS
Making their mark on the charts and in fans' hearts, Stray Kids are poised to lead the fourth generation to even greater heights.

CHAPTER 4

An Idol is Born

With such an established template for success in K-pop, it seemed inevitable that the next big thing would follow the same blueprint. But Stray Kids' subversion of the so-called K-pop formula is exactly what has made them stand out from the pack.

On the heels of creating all-girl sensation Twice via *Sixteen*, JYP Entertainment went back for seconds with a new show—this time with a twist. *Stray Kids*, which premiered in October 2017, followed the formation of a same-named all-male group as they wrote, choreographed, and performed their own music. The members worked together as a team and in subgroups to solidify their idol abilities. With each episode, a member could be at risk for elimination, leading to a nail-biting series of challenges and judgments.

To truly appreciate SKZ and their achievements, this show is required viewing. It shines a spotlight on what it truly takes to become an idol: the grueling trainee program and its rigorous practice schedules—not just songwriting, vocals, and dancing but also language skills and intangibles such as stage presence. It also highlights the interpersonal bonds that are so essential

to making or breaking a group, and the delicate combination of personalities and abilities required to make such complex machinery work.

The hopefuls on the show would all be trainees from within the JYPE system, but this time around, label head J. Y. Park wanted to try something different. Noting the desire for authenticity and true teamwork, he handed the reins to seasoned trainee Bang Chan, who would handpick the members and serve as their elder statesman and leader. He chose his 3RACHA cohorts Changbin and Han, along with fellow Aussie Felix, Lee Know, Seungmin, Hyunjin, rookie I.N, and Woojin. Over the course of 10 episodes, fans got to know the group members and their personalities, and form their own attachments and biases.

JYPE impresario J. Y. Park served as the main judge and talent evaluator, giving his unvarnished opinions about the performers' strengths and weaknesses. Contestants were vulnerable to elimination at the end of each episode, leading to fraught moments within the program. Lee Know was eliminated in episode 4 after mixing up his lyrics onstage. And Felix was eliminated in episode 8 for mistaken choreography and his continuing struggle with the Korean language. The eliminated members were brought back in the second-to-last episode, but with a caveat. The group would practice as a seven-member team and a nine-member team, each putting on a performance in the final episode. Fans would get to determine whether the group made its official debut with or without the eliminated members. The fans preferred the nine-member lineup and spared Lee Know and Felix from the jaws of elimination, with Park declaring, "I still see lacking parts in both of you, but when all nine perform, the expressions are alive. Congratulations. Stray Kids will debut as nine."

The group went quickly to work, releasing the music video for "Hellevator" immediately after the broadcast, when they already had a

DiD YoU KNoW?

The iconic Stray Kids logo was hand-drawn by none other than Bang Chan himself.

dedicated fan base waiting. The group's sound represented something new—something gritty, experimental, and even chaotic. Straight out of the gates, they were a polarizing force: you either loved them or you hated them—and that was totally okay with them.

After growing their profile with a number of musical releases, they returned to TV to compete against other idol groups on *Kingdom: Legendary War*. Their elaborately crafted performances earned them first place in the weekslong competition against better-known, more established groups including BTOB and iKON.

With comeback after comeback, STAY gets larger in number. But it's not just the music that keeps fans coming back. In addition to their incredible musical output, the group maintains an active and direct engagement with their fan base. Sidelined from performing during the pandemic, they seized the opportunity to connect with their fans in a different way: by creating a wealth of digital content. It's something they continue to this day, and their offerings run the gamut—skits, challenges, interviews, and behind-the-scenes peeks at their forthcoming projects, just to name a few. Bang Chan does a vlog called *Chan's Room*. And then there's *SKZ-PLAYER*, *SKZ CODE*, *SKZ-RECORD*, *TWO KIDS ROOM*, *THE 9TH*, *FINDING SKZ*, *SKZ-TALKER*, *SKZ GO*, *SKZ-PRACTICE ROOM*, *SPOT KIDS*, *HONEY-TIPS*, *CHOISKZ*...the list of

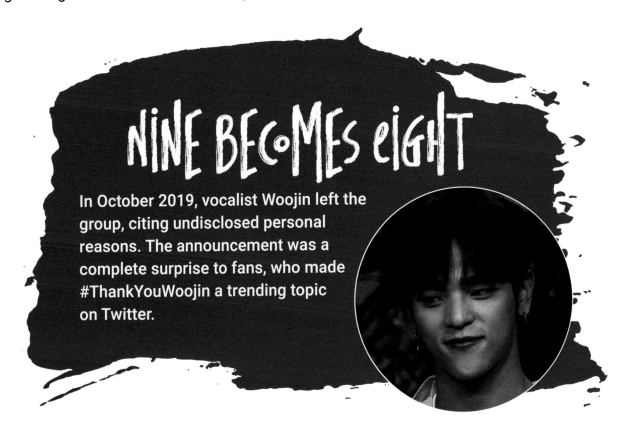

NINE BECOMES EIGHT

In October 2019, vocalist Woojin left the group, citing undisclosed personal reasons. The announcement was a complete surprise to fans, who made #ThankYouWoojin a trending topic on Twitter.

webisodes on and on. They also engage with fans on live broadcasts and via social media to give their fan base the most complete, all-access window into their lives as an idol group.

What can't be overstated is how integral each member's personality and talents are to the group's overall presentation. This lies in stark contrast to many K-pop groups, where synchronicity and polished, similarly dressed members are the norm. SKZ's individuality shines through in their appearances and performances, and even more important, it is a central hallmark of the music itself. "All eight of us have different preferences and tastes in music, so we can each bring a different color to the music we make," Changbin told Refinery29. "It lets our music be more diverse and it allows us to try new things."

Indeed, each member's contribution is essential to the overall makeup of the team. So without further ado, let's get acquainted with the Stray Kids! ●

TEST YOUR JYP IQ

Fans of the *Stray Kids* show know J. Y. Park, whom the members call by his initials JYP, all too well. Think of him as the Simon Cowell of South Korea; he's the mastermind behind JYP Entertainment and one of the most accomplished music executives in the business. But how well do you know Park? Here's a pop quiz.

1. True or false: Before starting a record label, Park was a K-pop performer.

2. What do the initials J. Y. stand for?
    A. Joon-young   B. Jin-young
    C. Jae-young   D. Just-young

3. True or false: Park was born in America but grew up in Korea.

4. Which of the following K-pop artists is not a Park protégé?
    A. GOT7   B. Rain
    C. Wonder Girls   D. EXO

5. Which one of the following is Park's nickname?
    A. The Asiansoul   B. Mr. President
    C. Godfather of K-pop   D. The Chairman

Answers

1) true; 2) b; 3) false—he was born and raised in Korea; 4) it's the boy band EXO; 5) a.

STRAY KIDS TV

While their debut survival show was the television program that propelled them to fame, Stray Kids have had plenty of amazing TV moments since then. Here's a list of 10 more must-see TV moments that endeared SKZ to members of STAY everywhere. And in case you missed them, you can catch each one of these stellar performances on YouTube.

January 16, 2018, *M Countdown*
Performing "Hellevator"—the song that started it all.

December 19, 2018, at the MAMA Awards
Winners of the fans' choice to perform, the group rose to the occasion, delivering a stunning, breakneck medley of their intro, "My Pace," "Hellevator," and "District 9" at the awards show.

April 14, 2019, on *M Countdown*
The boys nabbed their first music broadcast show win a scant year later. This performance of "Miroh" is one for the ages.

October 18, 2020, on *Inkigayo*
The boys turned up the *aegyo* to 11 on the competition stage, performing "Back Door."

May 19, 2021, on *Kingdom: Legendary War*
Their mash-up of "God's Menu" with BLACKPINK's "Ddu-du Ddu-du" helped solidify their dominance on the music competition show. They would take the crown after the following round.

2023 VMAs

March 18, 2022, on *The Late Show with Stephen Colbert*
The guys made their U.S. late-night debut on *Colbert*, performing "Maniac" and creating their own mania in the West.

November 29, 2022, at the MAMA Awards
The eye-popping visuals—complete with pyrotechnics, a human laboratory, and a four-story spider—made for an unforgettable performance that lasted nearly 10 minutes and left the audience breathless. It's their most watched live performance to date, with nearly 14 million views.

September 12, 2023, at the MTV 2023 Video Music Awards
The winners of that night's award for Best K-Pop Group made "S-Class" look more like a master class.

November 19, 2023, at the 2023 Billboard Music Awards
The group gave a 360-degree performance of "Lalalala" and "S-Class" and brought home BBMA honors in the process.

December 14, 2023, at the Asia Artist Awards
The guys gave a supersized performance, keeping up the energy through four separate songs—"Maniac," "Get Lit," "Topline," and "Lalalala"—all seemingly without breaking a sweat.

CHAPTER 5

Meet The Members

BANG CHAN

A self-described perfectionist whose work ethic cannot be matched, Bang Chan is the leader of the Stray Kids and their chief driving force. He plays a primary role in steering the direction of the music, but just as important, he serves to support the members and help them achieve their best. In this capacity, Bang Chan is a sterling role model for his *hyungs*, always quick with a hug or an encouraging word. The eldest of three siblings, he was born in South Korea and raised in Sydney, Australia. He learned his hardworking ways early as a dedicated student, musician, and athlete. He attended Newtown High School of the Performing Arts—a performing arts school known for famous alums, including Hugh Jackman—and in 2010, he passed the JYPE talent auditions in Australia and moved back to South Korea to become a trainee. He remained in the trainee system for several years, waiting in the wings as many of his friends made their debuts (including K-pop legends BamBam of GOT7, BLACKPINK's Lisa, and DAY6's Young K) while many others washed out of the system. Visionary, hyper-organized, and selfless, Bang Chan is deeply enmeshed in the industry and is a leading light in K-pop's fourth generation.

Producer

Leader

Mentor

3RACHA

VITAL STATS

Full name: Christopher Bahng

Born: October 3, 1997

Astrological signs: Libra + Ox

Nicknames: Chris, Kangaroo, Koala, CB97

Languages: He speaks English, Korean, and Japanese, and he is learning Chinese.

7: The number of years he spent as a trainee at JYPE. That's a long time by any measure, but of course the hard work paid off in the end!

Instruments: He plays the piano and guitar.

He's Sporty: He is a talented swimmer and soccer player.

Did You Know?: His hair is naturally curly.

Motto: It's advice his dad gave him: "Just enjoy."

He's an Overachiever: Groupmates say he gets about three to four hours of sleep per night—on a good day!

That's So Chan: "A compliment makes me feel really shy," he told *Teen Vogue* in 2022. "I'm thinking, am I allowed to accept it? When I look at myself, I'm not satisfied with myself yet."

Lee kNow

An only child, Lee Minho was born and raised in Gimpo, South Korea. His fellow members tease him for his 4D personality. (It's a distinctly Korean expression for someone who is lovably weird and who possesses the four dimensions of behavior, cognition, emotion, and motivation in equal measure.) He started dancing in middle school, and his skills attracted notice from JYPE, who offered him an audition...but then he never heard back. He got his big break in the industry as a backup dancer for superstars BTS, touring with the group in Japan. And then years after that first JYPE audition, he finally got the call and was added to their roster as a trainee. He's the leader of the DanceRacha and choreographs many of the group's routines. As anyone who's ever seen Stray Kids perform live can attest, his dancing chops are formidable. STAY stans Lee Know because of his good looks, fluid moves, and offbeat personality.

Dancer

Rapper

Vocalist

DanceRacha

VITAL STATS

Full name: Lee Minho

Born: June 22, 1987

Astrological signs: Scorpio + Tiger

Nicknames: Minho, Dancing Gem, Unreachable Visual

Languages: He speaks Korean, English, and Japanese.

2: The number of weeks it took him to pass the 40 phases of dance training at JYPE—reportedly the fastest-ever mark among trainees. (The previous mark was set at four *months*.)

Hobby: He is an avid boxer.

Hidden Talent: He is ambidextrous.

Animal Lover: He has three cats: Sooni, Doongi, and Dori.

Motto: "Let's eat well and live well."

Greatest Fear: He is afraid of heights.

Fun Fact: He loves watching superhero movies.

That's So Minho: "I joined JYPE the latest. I've always felt that the competitiveness is intense among trainees, but it's not like that in SKZ. It was like, 'Let's all debut together, fighting!' So I entered JYPE with a relaxed heart."

CHANGBIN

Changbin's interest in music developed as a child growing up in Uiwang and Seoul, where he learned to play violin at an early age. Later, he developed a fascination with hip-hop, and lists BIGBANG's G-Dragon as a formative influence on his music, along with American rapper Kendrick Lamar. As a main rapper for SKZ, his flow is legendary. He is widely recognized as the fastest rapper in K-pop. But while his flow is marked by a characteristic growl, he's also able to pull off vocals with a lighter, more sensitive touch. His fellow members tease him mercilessly about his eating habits, but however many sweet potatoes he might eat, he still looks lean. As a member of the 3RACHA, he produces the group's music under the name SPEARB. He's also one of the most encouraging members in the group, providing advice and motivation to his fellow *hyungs* and STAY alike.

Rapper
——————
Producer
——————
Lyricist
——————
3RACHA

VITAL STATS

Full name: Seo Changbin

Born: August 11, 1999

Astrological signs: Leo + Rabbit

Nicknames: Mogi, SPEARB, Lewis, Binnie, Baby

Languages: He speaks Korean, English, and Japanese.

11.13: The number of syllables Changbin can rap per second.

Sweet Secret: He sleeps every night with a cute plushy named Gyu.

He Gives Back: He is an active philanthropist who has supported causes ranging from LGBTQ+ rights to world hunger to disaster relief.

Fun Fact: Often seen sporting designer labels, he professes a love of shopping.

Hidden Talent: He is a skilled practitioner of tae kwon do.

Did You Know?: He never traveled on a plane until becoming an idol.

That's So Changbin: "I don't share a lot about myself, but music is like a channel that unravels these stories within me."

HYUNJIN

Hwang Hyunjin was born and raised in Seoul, and as a trainee he attended the prestigious School of Performing Arts Seoul (SOPA), where he studied ballet, jazz, and contemporary dance. The designated visual of the group, his fashion model looks also landed him a gig as a global ambassador for the luxury fashion brand Versace. In fact, it was his appearance that got him in the door at JYPE; a scout spotted him out shopping with his mom and invited him for an audition. But it was his skillful dancing and smooth voice that sealed the deal. He is a sensitive soul who looks for the beauty around him, and he expresses that through his music as well as other talents. He is a proficient artist who spends a lot of his downtime drawing and painting as well as taking photographs—and he often gives fans glimpses of his creations on social media. (His favorite thing to draw? Flowers.) He is also an avid reader of literature and poetry.

Dancer

Rapper

Vocalist

DanceRacha

VITAL STATS

Full name: Hwang Hyunjin

Born: March 20, 2000

Astrological signs: Pisces + Dragon

Nicknames: Jinnie, the Prince, Sam, Drama King

Languages: He speaks Korean and English.

Daily Ritual: He reads poetry every night before going to sleep.

Secret Habit: He talks in his sleep.

American Connection: He strengthened his English skills while living for a short time in Las Vegas, where he went by the name of Sam.

Puppy Love: He loves dogs! He has a long-haired Chihuahua named Kkami.

Did You Know?: Kkami was named after his former dog, Kkomi, whom he had as a boy. He wrote the song "Little Star" in the pooch's memory.

He Gives Back Too: Like some of his other groupmates, he is an active philanthropist with a passion for animal welfare and human rights.

Cool Collab: In 2023, he collaborated with Troye Sivan on the Aussie's single "Rush."

That's So Hyunjin: "I want to keep working harder and for us to keep doing better until we can all look back and ask ourselves, 'Wow, when did we get this far?'"

HAN

Though his musical gifts are abundant and evident, Han's family never expected him to be an idol. And in the end, he landed at JYP quite by accident. A friend encouraged him to tag along for an audition at the company. He almost didn't go, but his buddy suggested they might spot a celebrity or two. Convinced, Han agreed…and the rest is history. Soon after he met fellow trainees Bang Chan and Changbin, and 3RACHA was born. The trio started posting their collaborations on SoundCloud—the first of many dominoes to fall in the creation of SKZ. Han is known for his skills as a rapper and a vocalist. Many of the songs he has written for the group carry a common theme of self-empowerment. His inspirational words connect him to fans enduring their own struggles, large and small. In contrast to his deep and brooding lyrics, he has a lighthearted, sparkling personality and doesn't take himself too seriously.

Producer
——————
Rapper
——————
Vocalist
——————
3RACHA

VITAL STATS

Full name: Han Jisung

Born: September 14, 2000

Astrological signs: Virgo + Dragon

Nicknames: Squirrel, Donkey, J.ONE

Languages: He speaks Korean and English.

Instruments: He plays the guitar.

Weakness: He has a sweet tooth!

Hobbies: He is a huge fan of manga and anime.

Did You Know?: Though he was born in Korea, he spent most of his childhood in Malaysia.

Fun Fact: He was home-schooled.

Hidden Talent: Like groupmate Hyunjin, he is a talented illustrator.

Phobias: He has an unusual one—trypophobia. Seeing food or porous items full of holes gives him an extreme sense of revulsion.

That's So Han: "All we aspired to was spreading some warmth through our music, words of consolation and empathy with a community-oriented approach to music. I call it a vessel for communication with our audience and fans. Thanks to their warm reception and interactivity in response to our activities, we have formed a true sense of solidarity with STAYs."

Felix

Felix has one of the most recognizable voices in K-pop—a deep baritone that growls its way through song after song in the SKZ songbook. (Who can forget the opening of "Maniac," for instance?) But Felix is more than just a deep voice. He's got the vocal chops, dance skills, and idol good looks to back it up. Felix is one of two Aussies (along with Bang Chan) in the group, and his native English skills and confident demeanor make him a natural spokesperson for the group when they do appearances in the West. Felix found his way to JYPE after he and his friend were spotted by a talent scout on the street in Sydney, where they were invited to a local audition. His buddy didn't make the cut, but Felix soon found himself on a plane to Seoul, where he entered the trainee program. There he worked on honing his dancing and singing chops and brushed up on his rusty Korean skills. He is known for his warm, optimistic personality and continually goes out of his way to show his appreciation and support for his fellow members and STAY alike.

Dancer

Rapper

Vocalist

DanceRacha

VITAL STATS

Full name: Felix Lee

Korean name: Lee Yongbok

Born: September 15, 2000

Astrological signs: Virgo + Dragon

Nicknames: Haengbok (a play on the Korean word for happiness), Feelbok

Languages: He speaks Korean and English

Sports: He loves soccer.

Fun Fact: He's a clotheshorse—and a brand ambassador for the French luxury fashion house Louis Vuitton.

He's Super Sporty: He was a championship swimmer in Australia and is a third-degree black belt in tae kwon do.

63: The number of medals Felix has won in tae kwon do.

Hidden Talents: He likes to beatbox and draw.

Did You Know?: He has freckles.

That's So Felix: "As time goes by, STAY and Stray Kids are like a family. STAY, you are the greatest gift to us."

SEUNGMIN

Seungmin didn't always want to be an idol—but he did believe he was destined for greatness. Growing up, he had his sights trained on becoming a professional baseball player. He was good too—until injuries derailed his dream. Then a new dream came knocking. When Lee Daewhi, a friend of his who happened to be a trainee at JYPE, invited him to attend an open audition for the label, he jumped at the chance. He became a trainee himself, ultimately joining the Stray Kids in 2017 on their eponymous show. He worked hard to develop his vocal skills, and all that hard work paid off. When member Woojin left the band in 2019, Seungmin inherited most of Woojin's parts, many of which contained difficult high notes. Seungmin has assuredly stepped into the spotlight, handling his role of lead vocalist with grace and confidence.

He's a hard worker, but he also knows how to kick back, often cracking jokes and kidding his fellow members (especially *maknae* I.N).

Vocalist
_____
Dancer
_____
Rapper
_____
VocalRacha

VITAL STATS

Full name: Kim Seungmin

Born: September 22, 2000

Astrological signs: Virgo + Dragon

Nicknames: Snail, Sunshine, Puppy, Sky

Languages: He speaks Korean and English.

How Neat: He is known for his cleanliness—no small virtue when living with a bunch of guys in a trainees' dorm.

American Connection: He learned how to speak English while living briefly in Los Angeles.

Hidden Talents: He likes to cook. He also is excellent at rapping in English (check out "Maze of Memories" for one example).

Fun Fact: He won his first music award in grade school, taking home a prize for singing a nursery rhyme.

Scary Story: When he was a boy, a helicopter crashed into the building where he lived while he was standing there brushing his teeth. Yikes!

He's Disciplined: The *Stray Kids* program described him as an "icon of diligence" due to his strict training regimen. He kept exhaustive diaries during his time as a trainee, never missing a day—or a chance to improve.

That's So Seungmin: "We usually don't compare [ourselves] to others…. When [we say] we don't care about others' [achievements], we're just talking about Stray Kids' own way."

I.N

Just as the eldest in the group has a role (as leader—and Bang Chan is an exemplary one for SKZ), so does the youngest. And I.N fulfills the role of *maknae* well, learning from and being solicitous to his fellow members. Within K-pop circles, he's also referred to as "Maknae on Top," a nod to the satirical track by the same name that I.N released, where he lords over his groupmates, but also a recognition of his prowess as a vocalist and performer. But he wasn't always so confident. He learned how to sing as a child while in church, and often performed trot music for the elders in his congregation. Impressed by his clear talent, they encouraged him to audition as a singer, which led him to JYPE and the prestigious School of Performing Arts Seoul. Shy and serious, this *maknae* has an old soul—though he's quick with a one-liner when the situation calls for it!

Vocalist

Dancer

Maknae

VocalRacha

VITAL STATS

Full name: Yang Jeongin

Born: February 8, 2001

Astrological signs: Aquarius + Snake

Nicknames: Desert Fox, Baby Bread, Bean Worm

Languages: He speaks Korean.

Model Behavior: He worked as a fashion model when he was a child.

Hobby: He's a big fan of watching ASMR videos.

Hidden Talent: His ability to sing trot (a traditional form of Korean singing, short for "foxtrot").

American Idol: Bruno Mars is his biggest musical influence and role model.

Did You Know?: He wore braces for years, finally getting them off in 2019.

Guilty Pleasure: He's a big fan of watching Korean *mukbang*, a type of online eating show.

Fun Fact: He's way into meditation.

That's So I.N: "Let's have a good time!"

CHAPTER 6

Behind The Music

The DIY aesthetic that Stray Kids puts into their music is their hallmark. From day one, JYP has taken a hands-off approach with the group, letting the members do their own thing. It all starts with 3RACHA—Bang Chan, Changbin, and Han—who write and produce most of the music that the group performs. Together they created a sound that is incomparable to anything else going in K-pop today—a wild, exuberant and, by all measures, *loud* mixture of disparate genres. "The goal is to continuously pioneer new [musical] subjects and to have our music be recognized as a 'Stray Kids' genre," Changbin told *Time* magazine in 2023.

The Korean media first coined the term "mala taste" to describe their sound. It's inspired by the Chinese numbing soup *malatang*, a complex concoction that is as super-spicy as it is addictive. That "spicy" moniker makes perfect sense. As a matter of fact, the 3RACHA trio took their name from "-racha," as in the spicy sauce Sriracha, and injected that into their music from the get-go. The trio of Bang Chan, Changbin, and Han has been making music together since their

"**Stray Kids has their own distinct color and...we're artists who can apply our musical color to anything, regardless of genre.**"

—Han to *NME*

trainee days, posting their experimental creations on SoundCloud under the names CB97, J.ONE, and SPEARB.

Using the no-rules spirit of 3RACHA as their musical guidepost, Stray Kids have carved out a niche all their own. And as time has gone on, they've only leaned into that identity as outsiders. When naysayers said they were too noisy, they doubled down, releasing an album called *Noeasy*. When haters called them too spicy, they met them head-on with "God's Menu," boasting, "all our dishes taste so strong." Many of their songs speak directly to the conviction they have for their music. But it's not all braggadocio. Other songs speak directly to the heavy emotional toll of being young—anxiety, self-doubt, and the weight of criticism and expectations. It's

this relatability that's played a large part in connecting them with fans.

"People can distinguish who has sincerity in their music," JYP executive Shannen Song told *Billboard* in 2023. "That's the biggest strength for their music and for them."

They've also benefited from a business arrangement that has afforded them an opportunity to take their work to audiences in the West. In 2020, JYPE partnered with American music label Republic Records, who believe that SKZ's edge gives them a leg up in cracking the American market. So far, that instinct has been right on.

But while the group has broken the mold in some ways with their music,

HOW TO SPEAK K-POP

comeback

Whether it's a single, an EP, or a full-length album, K-pop fans don't have long to wait for new music from their bias. Each new release is called a comeback.

3RACHA onstage at the 2023 Global Citizen Concert.

they still retain plenty of qualities that define the K-pop idol. You'll still find the crisp visuals and razor-sharp choreography, the catchy hooks, and the flirtatious performances. You'll also see them follow the same trajectory as their fellow K-pop artists where it comes to releasing new music. Unlike the American pop industry, where fans generally hope to get one album from their favorite artist each year, *if they're*

lucky—K-pop artists are a different breed, releasing comeback after comeback throughout the calendar year.

The following discography touches on Stray Kids' main releases—EPs and full-length albums. To list every single, Japanese release, repackage, and compilation would make this book much longer. But it's all worth a listen! ●

MIXTAPE
Released January 8, 2018

1. **Hellevator**
2. Beware (Grrr)
3. Spread My Wings
4. YAYAYA
5. Glow
6. School Life
7. 4419

"Hellevator" is a metaphor for the emotional ups and downs young people suffer. Stray Kids' first single, it was intended as a beacon to reach "stray kids" everywhere.

"*Hellevator* has the brooding atmosphere down, casting the group in an oddly moody light…. Hard-hitting and aggressive in production and performance…the track strings together several tropes, from the cathartic rap style to the pensive vocal pre-chorus, to the 'drop' that makes up the actual hook…. Being from JYP Entertainment, they're almost guaranteed a certain level of success. They'd be wise to take that platform and push the genre forward, rather than keep it stuck in neutral."—The Bias List

I AM NOT
Released March 25, 2018

1. NOT!
2. **District 9**
3. Mirror
4. Awaken
5. Rock
6. Grow Up
7. 3rd Eye
8. Mixtape #1

SKZ defined their own unique territory, calling it **"District 9"** (for its then-nine-member outfit). This song showcases their ability to meld different genres, including EDM, hip-hop, and rock.

"One should not be fooled by the fact that they go by the name 'kids' as *I am NOT* is one of the roughest albums of the year so far. Combining hard rock sounds with rap is an unusual choice in K-pop nowadays but it may actually play in their favor in building a distinctive sound of their own…. While in several idol groups the rapper tends to generally be someone who is not particularly talented in singing and/or has a lower voice range, the rappers in Stray Kids know exactly what they are doing…. [A] solid debut album for a rookie group [that] showcases different sides of the group while still keeping consistency in sound…. Stray Kids definitely have a promising career ahead."—Seoulbeats

I AM WHO?
Released August 6, 2018

1. WHO?
2. My Pace
3. **Voices**
4. Question
5. Insomnia
6. M.I.A.
7. Awkward Silence
8. Mixtape #2

Dragging the feelings of self-doubt into the light, **"Voices"** is a call to banish them once and for all.

"You can see how honest they are in their music, and the fact that nearly all of the members are involved in their music and songwriting really showcases that.... Listening to this album was like having a good cry and then slowly getting back on your feet afterwards."—Amino Apps

I AM YOU
Released October 22, 2018

1. You.
2. **I Am You**
3. My Side
4. Hero's Soup
5. Get Cool
6. N/S
7. 0325
8. Mixtape #3

Full of optimism and encouragement, this love letter to STAY is tailor-made for a motivational playlist.

"*I am YOU* is a stimulating, emotive take on rap-heavy electro-pop and revels in dramatic guitar riffs and hi-hat heavy beats. It, like all of the album's tracks, was co-written by the group's trio of songwriters 3RACHA...and lyrically explores the relationship between two people who find themselves in one another."—*Billboard*

CLÉ 1: MIROH
Released March 25, 2019

1. Entrance
2. Miroh
3. Victory Song
4. Maze of Memories
5. Boxer
6. **Chronosaurus**
7. 19
8. Mixtape #4

Personifying anxiety as a fierce "time dinosaur," **"Chronosaurus"** encourages listeners to keep moving forward without fear of what lies ahead.

"Stray Kids throws you intensity right, left, and center."
—KpopReviewed.com

CLÉ 2: YELLOW WOOD
Released June 19, 2019

1. **Road Not Taken**
2. Side Effects
3. TMT
4. Mixtape #1
5. Mixtape #2
6. Mixtape #3
7. Mixtape #4

Inspired by Robert Frost's famous poem "The Road Not Taken," SKZ urges listeners to consider taking the road less traveled rather than the one that seems preordained for them.

"The disorienting song structure, the psychedelic genre they've tapped into, plus a brilliant sample of what sounds like a monotone, prescription-medicine ad listing-off 'common side effects,' all blend together to create the type of messy portrait of a young person coming into their own in 2019. But instead of try to polish the mess away, the guys embrace such a chaotic nature like some of the best young artists are today."—*Billboard*

CLÉ: LEVANTER
Released December 10, 2019

1. Stop
2. Double Knot
3. **Levanter**
4. Booster
5. Astronaut
6. Sunshine
7. You Can Stay
8. Mixtape #5

Check out the music video—it's full of tons of Easter eggs for fans familiar with the group's previous work.

"Only Stray Kids know where their compass will lead them next. But if the *Clé* series, for all of its ambitious musicality and maturity, is emblematic of their future direction, then it's a course worth charting."—MTV

GO LIVE
Released June 17, 2020

1. Go Live
2. **God's Menu**
3. Easy
4. Pacemaker
5. Airplane
6. Another Day
7. Phobia
8. Blueprint
9. Ta
10. Haven
11. Top
12. Slump
13. Mixtape: Gone Days
14. Mixtape: On Track

Time magazine hailed it as one of the best songs of the year, describing **"God's Menu"** as "an artful Frankenstein that's as catchy as it is complex."

"*Go Live* (2020) represents a turning point in Stray Kids' sound. As the first track off the album of the same name, Stray Kids decide to do a complete U-turn, switching out their familiar hard-hitting song with an abrasive electronic, almost techno influenced track…. The slight nods to the group's previous work makes the song almost nostalgic."—*Clash* magazine

IN LIFE
Released September 14, 2020

1. The Hare and the Tortoise
2. **Back Door**
3. B Me
4. Any
5. Ex
6. We Go
7. Wow
8. My Universe
9. God's Menu
10. Easy
11. Pacemaker
12. Airplane
13. Another Day
14. Phobia
15. Blueprint
16. Ta
17. Haven

One of the new tracks on the repackaged album, **"Back Door,"** is pure enjoyment, inviting listeners behind the velvet rope and into an exclusive engagement. The shifting visuals and extremely technical choreography in the accompanying music video show a more polished side of SKZ than ever before.

"The [eight] new releases are some of Stray Kids' most unique and charismatic songs [to date]."—AllKpop

---

NOEASY
Released August 23, 2021

1. Cheese
2. Thunderous
3. Domino
4. Ssick
5. The View
6. Sorry, I Love You
7. **Silent Cry**
8. Secret Secret
9. Star Lost
10. Red Lights
11. Surfin'
12. Gone Away
13. Wolfgang
14. Mixtape: Oh

"Thunderous" and "Wolfgang" were the lead singles here, but **"Silent Cry,"** a tender depiction of depression and anxiety, shows a different side of the group.

"Stray Kids perfect their ability to make even the quiet parts unabashedly loud, showing us how to live with the noise—not run away from it."—*Teen Vogue*

ODDINARY
Released March 19, 2022

1. Venom
2. **Maniac**
3. Charmer
4. Freeze
5. Lonely St.
6. Waiting For Us
7. Muddy Water

One of their most commercially popular songs to date, it was named one of the best songs of the year by *Rolling Stone*, *Billboard*, and *NME*, among other prestigious publications.

"This mini-album is a reflection of their extraordinary passion, wit, and growth. It's an elegant step forward for a group who, hopefully, will never get tired of raising questions."—*NME*

MAXIDENT
Released October 7, 2022

1. **Case 143**
2. Chill
3. Give Me Your TMI
4. Super Board
5. 3Racha
6. Taste
7. Can't Stop
8. Circus (Korean ver.)

A not-so-subtle code for I L-O-V-E Y-O-U, this action-packed music video launches a literal investigation into the things we do for love.

"*Maxident* is an experimental release even for Stray Kids, an eruption of creative chaos in the most captivating manner…. By utilizing their strengths as a self-produced group, they shine brighter with every comeback as their impact on the industry grows."—*Disrupted* magazine

5-STAR
Released June 2, 2023

1. Hall of Fame
2. **S-Class**
3. Item
4. Super Bowl
5. Topline
6. DLC
7. GET LIT
8. Collision
9. FNF
10. Youtiful
11. The Sound (Korean Ver.)
12. Mixtape : Time Out

Using the luxury car as a metaphor for their own high style, **"S-Class"** is supported by a sprawling music video that showcases the group's love for blockbuster action movies.

"On first listen, the third studio album from Stray Kids will make you feel like you arrived at a party that's already in full swing—the atmosphere is electric if not a little intoxicating, the air thick with lively chatter and heavy bass that thumps in your chest, while you wander from room to room trying to find your bearings. *5-Star* is disorienting in that way. But once your senses adapt to the frenzy and your body syncs to the rhythm, you lose yourself in its luminescence…. Stray Kids are flying so high above the crowd that they're in a galaxy of their very own, where the parties are endless and the vibes are always five-star."—*NME*

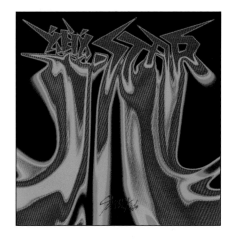

ROCK-STAR
Released November 10, 2023

1. Megaverse
2. **Lalalala**
3. Blind Spot
4. Comflex
5. Cover Me
6. Leave
7. Social Path
8. Lalalala (Rock version)

This was the first Stray Kids single to crack Billboard's Hot 100 but certainly will not be the last.

"With a variety of perspectives, ROCK-STAR finds Stray Kids broadening their creative palette while revisiting their more rebellious roots."—*Teen Vogue*

"There's no answer to music. It's all about preference.... We're unique and experimental, that could be a reason why opinions are so polarizing, but as long as we like it, and if there are people out who like it the same way as we like it, then it's a win-win situation."

—Bang Chan to *GQ Australia*

CHAPTER 7

They Make Stray Kids Stay

Fans in Miami turned out for their idols with custom merchandise and personalized messages in Korean.

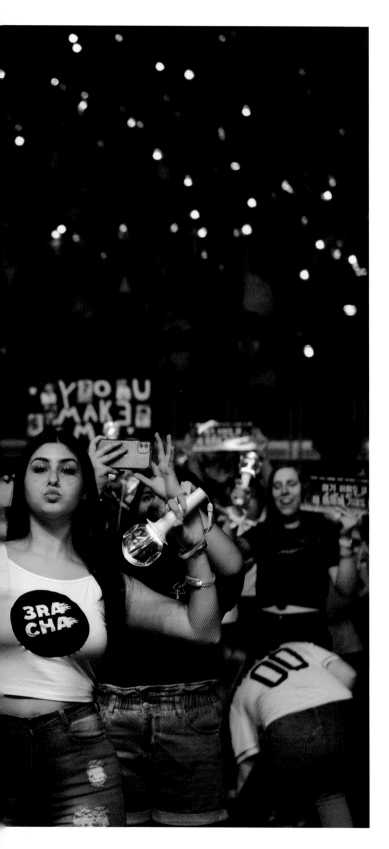

Fans of K-pop exhibit a

tribalism that rivals that of any musical genre. They are fierce, loyal, and extensively involved in their chosen idol's every move. But more important than that, they are a community unto themselves: a group of individuals who not only lift up the artist but support and elevate one other with the same vigor. STAY is no exception. Their community is open and involved, whether it's spreading the word about upcoming events and releases, answering questions from newcomers, disseminating fan chants and other resources for live performances, or combining efforts to get their group to the top. Further, the culture is one of inclusivity and understanding, a place where everyone is welcome.

And that's exactly what Stray Kids had in mind from the very beginning. When it came time to choose their name, this spirit of inclusivity was their guiding principle. They wanted to create a home for their listeners: "Our goal ever since we debuted was to reach as many 'stray kids' as possible, to deliver our music and give strength to people who really need it," Bang Chan told *Billboard* in 2023. It's the idea that their fans are

like family, a sentiment that is repeated often by the group and fans alike.

For a typical K-pop group, the label would be in charge of such things as creating the name of the group, its image, song selection...even the name of its fan base. But in this too, the

group came up with the acronym STAY themselves. As Felix explained to New York's Z100, "The reason why it is 'STAY,' from Stray Kids we take out the *R* from *Stray*, and it becomes STAY. The *R* is the reason why STAY is here with us."

Ask any STAY why they follow the group, and they're ready with a million reasons. For some, it's the relatability of their songs, which often feel like a direct dialogue with listeners. For others, it's their inimitable, over-the-top performance style, or their accessibility and the way they interact with fans. And for many, it doesn't hurt that they're easy on the eyes too.

Their appeal extends to celebrity admirers as well. Back in 2021, the group's *Deadpool*-inspired set piece for their performance of "God's Menu"/ "Ddu-du Ddu-du"

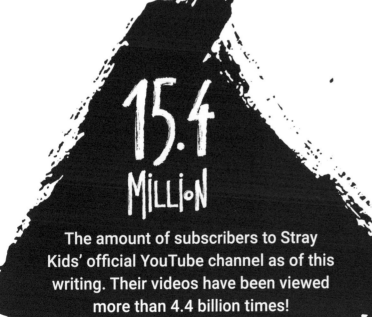

15.4 MILLION

The amount of subscribers to Stray Kids' official YouTube channel as of this writing. Their videos have been viewed more than 4.4 billion times!

on *Kingdom: Legendary War* caught the attention of Deadpool himself, actor Ryan Reynolds, who declared leader Bang Chan his "new favorite Australian." Australian actor and onscreen Wolverine Hugh Jackman also follows the superhero-loving group on social media.

"You made Stray Kids stay," is a rallying cry for the fandom and the group's unofficial motto. It is often repeated by the group and serves as a de facto sign-off in music videos and performances, and on social media. Whether in their music, online, or in live performance, the group goes out of their way to make sure they show their fans love. That connection is mutual and deeply held. It's a concept that Koreans call *jeong*—a sort of invisible thread linking them all together.

The group and their fandom are inextricably tied, halves of a whole. "A long time ago, I told STAY that I wanted to make them proud of being STAY, but now I have changed my mind. I am proud to be Stray Kids because of STAY," said Lee Know.

The audience goes wild for Stray Kids at Lollapalooza Paris in 2023.

HOW TO SPEAK K-POP

Entering the K-pop landscape can be overwhelming. With an abundance of abbreviations, inside jokes, and Korean vocabulary, there's a lot to learn. The following is a glossary of handy terms every stan should know in order to communicate with idols and fellow fans.

aegyo: Acting flirtatious or cutesy, it's especially associated with the flirtatious onstage behavior of idol groups. I.N's got it in spades with his eye smile.

aigoo: It's an interjection used in surprise, frustration, or chastisement, meaning, basically, "Oops."

all-rounder: Think of it as a jack-of-all-trades. It's an idol who can do it all: sing, dance, and rap. SKZ's Han fits this mold.

an moo: Choreography. It's universally considered an essential element of any idol group.

andwae: No way! As in, "Did Stray Kids just debut another album at No. 1? *Andwae!*"

annyeong: This one's a twofer—it means both hello *and* goodbye.

assa: Woo-hoo!

be peu: Like "BFF," it's an abbreviation meaning "best friend."

bi dam: The most attractive member in a group.

bias: Your favorite member within a group.

chingu: Friend.

choom: Dance.

comeback: Think of it more like "follow-up." It's a term used to describe a group's latest musical output. Whenever a new release is issued, it's the group's comeback.

daebak: Awesome.

dongsaeng: Meaning younger brother or sister, it can be used to refer to anyone younger than oneself.

eye smile: A key weapon in any idol's arsenal, a powerful eye smile is the ultimate *aegyo*.

fighting: Used to cheer on your idols, it's like saying "Go get 'em!"

ganji: Stylish, trendy, fashionable—your everyday, ordinary swag.

gayo: Another name for K-pop.

geumsabba: If you've fallen in love at first sight, this word describes you!

gomawo: Thank you.

gwiyomi: Slang term for someone adorable or cute, often a child.

haeng syo: An informal way to say goodbye, roughly translating to "Peace out."

hoobae: Meaning "junior," it's a respectful term of address for someone younger/more inexperienced than you.

hul: Next time you want to type "I can't even…" try this instead, roughly meaning "whoa."

hyung: Older brother, but can be used to refer to a close friend as well.

idol: It's a term used to describe a K-pop group—kinda like the American equivalent of rock star.

jebal: Please.

jjang: Alternately, awesome or the very best.

jon jal: Incredibly good-looking, when referring to a male—as in, "My, is Hyunjin *jon jal!*"

king wang jjang: If you love Stray Kids infinity squared, try this phrase on for size. It doesn't get any more superlative than this, meaning the absolute best.

Koreaboo: A person who has a strong affinity for all things Korean.

maknae: Youngest member of a group; in SKZ's case, I.N.

manleb: Next level. This is the word you use to describe someone whose skills are way beyond their peers'. (Any ideas, STAY?)

maum: Emotions, or heart. Warning: a *maum* can be stolen!

mi nam: A handsome guy.

mwongi: The Korean version of "WTF?!"

nam chin: Boyfriend.

omo: Short for *omona*, it means "Oh, my!"

oppa: Older brother, or any male older than oneself.

ottoke: An expression of confusion or exasperation that means "What to do?" As in, "OMG, Stray Kids are playing the same day as Taylor Swift. *Ottoke?*"

sa rang hae: I love you.

saesang: An overly obsessive fan…but not in a good way.

sangnamja: A manly man. As in, "Look at Bang Chan's muscles—what a *sangnamja!*"

selca: Selfie.

shim koong: Like the feeling you might get seeing your first SKZ concert, it means your heart is beating a mile a minute.

simkung: Translating roughly to "heartthrob," this is how you can refer to your bias.

SKZ: The abbreviated version of Stray Kids.

stan: This originated with Eminem's song of the same name, about a violently obsessive fan, though it's come to mean a fan who is devoted in a good way!

sunbae: Meaning "senior," it's an honorific that members of Stray Kids would use to address, say, J. Y. Park.

ulzzang: A combination of *face* and *best*, it is a superlative used to describe a particularly handsome guy.

utpudah: What lies at the intersection of laughter and tears.

visual: This term describes the look of the group, how the performance appears onstage. It can also describe the member designated to be the face of the group, often the most attractive.

yeo chin: Girlfriend.

You make Stray Kids stay: The official motto of STAY, and a phrase SKZ often uses as a sign-off on their videos.

4419: This number references an early SKZ song, titled after the bus that Bang Chan used to ride during his trainee days. The number has significance among STAY, who hold celebrations every April 4 in commemoration. (Fun fact: Stray Kids also won their first music competition show on 4/4/19!)

CHAPTER 8

What's
Next

When asked about their

accomplishments, Stray Kids stay humble. "To be honest, accomplishing [what we have] still makes me wonder if I'm dreaming or if I'm still just not in my reality," Felix told the Grammys in 2023. "Every time I think about it, I'm still so surprised that I have to look at the amount of comments our STAY have left just to believe it. Truly, it's a huge gift from STAY everywhere around the world."

As for the goals they have for the future, they characteristically bring it back to their fans. "I hope we're able to have a positive effect on all of those who listen to our music," Seungmin told the Grammys in 2023. "Like, when people listen to our music in the far future, they'll be able to vividly remember all of the memories from the past. I want to show everyone the awesome power of music."

There's no telling what the future will bring for SKZ, but considering their commitment to their craft and STAY's commitment to them, the sky's the limit. With a world tour, another fan meeting, and two new albums in the offing for 2024, it's safe to say that there's much more to come. ●

Library of Congress Cataloging-in-Publication Data is available upon request.

This book is available in quantity at special discounts for your group or organization. For further information, contact:
   Triumph Books LLC
   814 North Franklin Street, Chicago, Illinois 60610
   (312) 337-0747 | www.triumphbooks.com

Printed in U.S.A.
ISBN: 978-1-63727-657-0

Design by Patricia Frey; edited by Laine Morreau